L(EYE)GHT

Jessica Kim

Advance Praise for L(EYE)GHT

"That English allows for metaphors of 'sight' to so commonly signify 'understanding' is a great shame of the language. Jessica Kim's *L(EYE)GHT* is not only a reminder of that shame but also an indictment of it, an answer in verse to the speaker's own wondering 'if her optic nerves / lead to an inheritance'—yes, an inheritance Kim graciously lays bare in vivid poems of abundance. 'The eye doctor shines / a light into my eyes and I'm afraid / he can trace the dream / I had last night.' Our tracing of that dream and mind is the gift this collection offers, knowledge that lies only outside the eye's 'facade of illusion.'"
—Mario Chard,
author of *Land of Fire* (Tupelo Press)

"The poems in this collection invite us to 'unsee' and 'unlearn' alongside the speaker as she moves from not wanting to talk about her disability to embracing it. 'Someday, I will tell my disability / I'd want to keep her in my next life,' Jessica Kim writes in the final poem. Using a variety of free and received forms, Kim takes us from a Korean supermarket and an optometrist's office in California to the streets of Prague and Seoul. With a wide-reaching scope and such rich language, this chapbook has me hooked. I can't wait to read more books by Jessica Kim!"
—Katie Manning,
author of *How to Play* (Louisiana Literature Press)

"'To renounce a language / that cannot differentiate mother from a body' is Jessica Kim's attentive and careful work. Kim's *L(EYE)GHT* is populated by women who have survived the imperial violence that renders places like home illegible. Kim demands we see them—the daughters, mothers, and grandmothers. These are poems to wade into ('summertime up to our waistlines') with your hands out, ready to confront the ways we may be 'loved / and nothing more.'"
—C. T. Salazar,
author of *Headless John the Baptist Hitchhiking* (Acre Books)

"In *L(EYE)GHT*, Jessica Kim mines the senses, memory, and 'muscle-movement of a mother tongue' to supplement her sight. Her poems engage rich, textured versions of herself in her mother's language, the optometrist's office with vitreous ghosts, and the supermarket's labyrinth. These long-awaited debut poems shift easily with Kim's curiosity, her reinventions of and experiences in changing environments making and remaking who she is becoming."
—Ashaki M. Jackson,
author of *LANGUAGE LESSON* (Miel)

"'Now, I steal / into the party dressed as Asian and / disabled. Someone inquires where's / your costume.' Jessica Kim's chapbook *L(EYE)GHT* sets her Korean-American and visually-impaired identities in front of an urban Los Angeles backdrop and explores them through myriad poetic forms. These poems are self-portraits told in a powerful voice—one that notices everything, and forces us to notice, 'The cashier plastic wraps the fish thrice.' A stunning chapbook from an emerging poet to watch."
—Jessica Abughattas,
author of *Strip* (University of Arkansas Press)

L(EYE)GHT

Jessica Kim

Copyright © 2022 Jessica Kim

All Rights Reserved. This book or any portion thereof may not be reproduced, in whole or in part, in any form (beyond that permitted by Sections 107 and 108 of the U.S Copyright Law and except by reviewers for the public press), without the express written permission of the publisher except for the use of brief quotations in a book review.

Kim, Jessica / author

L(EYE)GHT / Jessica Kim

Poems

ISBN: 978-1-7365167-7-5

Edited by: Beth Gordon
Book Design: Amanda McLeod
Cover Art: Miye Sugino
Cover Design: Amanda McLeod

PUBLISHER
Animal Heart Press
P.O. Box 322
Thetford Center, Vermont 05075
www.animalheartpress.net

"You once told me that the human eye is god's loneliest creation."
— Ocean Vuong

Table of Contents

POEM IN WHICH I DO NOT TALK ABOUT MY DISABILITY	13
SHATTERED	14
BRAILLET	16
WHAT NOT TO EXPECT AT A KOREAN SUPERMARKET	17
FISH-BODIED	18
SUPERMARKET HORSE	19
POEM IN WHICH I CANNOT DRIVE	20
DEUS EX MACHINA	21
OF THE WORLDS YOU CAN NAME	23
POEM IN WHICH I TALK ABOUT MY DISABILITY	24
ENCOUNTER DURING NIGHT OF DEATH	25
SKEDADDLE FOR BLIND GIRL	26
HAIBUN FOR EVERYTHING THAT DIES THIS SUMMER	27
GHAZAL FOR K	28
DISAPPEARING ACT	29
OCCLUDER	30
MONOCHROMACY	31
FIREWORK GIRLS	32
FACELESS ELEGY	34
THERE IS NO RENAISSANCE HERE	36

IN A DREAM, WE ALL LOSE OUR SIGHT	37
POEM IN WHICH MY DISABILITY TALKS ABOUT ME	38
ACKNOWLEDGEMENTS	41
ABOUT THE AUTHOR	43

POEM IN WHICH I DO NOT TALK ABOUT MY DISABILITY

Before I was all pigmented and luminous,
there were signposts with faces of girls.
In the backseat, I watch the city compress
their bodies into buildings. Their limbs

contorted by an alchemy of creation and
transition. I ghost-walk the city at sundown,
when there is nothing left worth window-
shopping for. After staring at commercials

about eyeglasses, I little myself into street
crowds. Trade an eye for an eye, foresee ill-
fated accidents. While wearing my own
eyeglasses, I cannot differentiate sky from

skyscrapers, museums from churches.
A refractive error. Everything requires
sight: cinemas, nightclubs, even sight-
seeing. I avoid confrontation with

my eyes. I'm talking about everything
except that. I teeter across subway carriages,
bumping into multiple metal poles.
        Only seeing a girl's face, disabled.

SHATTERED
after Sally Wen Mao

I move to California, but no one recognizes
my chipped face—graffiti across the subway station,
a self-portrait eroded by the plastic coating on
my green card. In 1903, the first wave of Korean
immigrants flooded America, their faces plasticized
with sugarcane, pinchfuls of copper pennies,
images of a merciless God. On Sundays, they file
into the only church in town: eyes lowered, lips
sealed, hands clutching a pocket-sized bible.
A conversion factor that divides forgiver from
foreigner. I no longer recognize the yellowed face
on my card—though I finger its creases and trace
the route back to motherland. I am alone in the city
of Los Angeles, skin peeling from my face like
wrinkled posters at the metro station. There's a full-
body snapshot of a white girl, the next Hollywood
star, staring at me in the eye like I'm the villain's
abandoned sidekick. For a split second, my reflection
matches hers, vanishing before I can capture its
perfection: like the year mother shoved me into
a suitcase and sold me to the white man in another
city. In another shade of gray cement, in another
wavelength of a car honk, I forget to live. I assume
no one will come searching for me at a starving
downtown restaurant. I'm not even hungry,
but I nibble at the grains of rice without noticing.
The grains stuck to the left pocket of the shirt-
dress I bought in Namdaemun market. I want to
escape this hunger for home—or model myself
into the poster girl, the picture of God that begs me
to leave America: to spit out a currency for empty
distances. It begs me to unwrite this poem—
erase the tenderness of Christianity, picture brides,

exclusion. I'm on the last metro for the night,
heading for Union station, a sputter from
my larynx. America, even if I can speak in frag-
ments for imported faces without names,
they do not answer—I am still a stranger here.

BRAILLET

It's almost too easy to see in the dark / when you can't see at all in the first place. / The moon blinking without eyes. / You can feel the granular refraction / of light in the white space of your eyes, / engraved as raised dots. Each speck as / its own spotlight. It's almost too unreal, / how your fingers pirouette across / braille books, the bumps an aching / for possibility. What could have been. / Outside, you can hear the next-door / neighbor blasting party tunes. / It's interrupting your ballet repertoire. / Already, the once-raised dots / have faded from its pages. Now, / a memorial for those worn-out hands, / those untouched eyes. You grope for / the light switch and can't tell if / it's already on. Below the halogen / light bulb, you are spiraling on the same dot.

WHAT NOT TO EXPECT AT A KOREAN SUPERMARKET

Now watch me strangle the neck of the apricot tree,
        watch me grab a back of green onions and cage it in
the rusty supermarket cart. Like the flight here from California,
        confined in the small body of an aircraft.
The Korean peninsula devours my body and swallows.
        I wonder why I am so welcomed but there's no time
to think. I scan the grocery list: garlic cloves, jujubes,
        ginseng roots, anything exotic for an American tongue.
What can I do, except circle the labyrinth's endless aisles
        of packaged heartbreaks? I walk around until my soles
become flaps of rice paper and I tape them back
        onto my shoes with sticky plastic wrappers so that
no one will think of me as an intruder. I throw a pack of ginseng
        into the cart, then run into a cul-de-sac of fermented fish
bodies. The corner smells like ammonia, but what
        can I do, except blockade my nostrils? What can I do,
but slab the dead meat on the cashier just to look Korean
        enough? All eyes turn to the repulsive deadness.
I barely have enough money from the last time I visited the country
        and the coupons in my wallet have expired the year before.
The cashier plastic-wraps the fish thrice to preserve my decision
        and I scurry out to the back parking lot, burning
red like chili, only to remember that I forgot to buy the jujubes.
        I do nothing, except fabricate an excuse.
I tell myself I'm still a good person, and every good person
        returns home. What can I do anyways?
I do nothing, except gallop across potholes on charred
        pavement, ignore the whiff of sweet Korean pancakes
frosting in my mouth? What could I be, a suppressed
        version of American? I should be—

FISH-BODIED

In Korean, *mom* means *body*. I imagine a body
shaped like a raw jeon-uh, silver-skinned but small
like a daughter without a homeland. To survive,
I memorize the muscle-movement of a mother
tongue, watching mother's swollen lips waver across
a foreign coast. Words unmouthed like broken
apologies thrown out to sea. See, in my language, *uh*
means *fish;* in another, it is the dehydrated whimper
of mother on her deathbed. She clutches my palms
in a plea for me to return home and I understand now,
that han-guk was never mine to begin with. I forget
how to translate death into elegies; I instead liken
mother to a jeon-uh, grayed and dried out, unable to
live longer than two days in a water tank. The country
a cage of self-destruction. I pick at its ripened scales,
then admire its upturned belly, whitened by the bygone
summer. It is early autumn: not a season for death,
but completion. Mother chews a jeon-uh in its entirety,
both flesh and bone meshing into cremated ashes.
I choose to dispose of its softened skeleton, to cleanse
away this sickening obsession, to renounce a language
that cannot differentiate mother from a body.

SUPERMARKET HORSE
after Ada Limon

Born girl and horse. Grandmother at
        the supermarket, persistently shoving

omens on my palms: bad luck. Tell me
        again, *horse bad for women.* She aims

for the vegetables, onions and cabbage
        slapped into the cart, greased with mettle

and augury. I yearn for meat. The aisles
        endless with too many scraps of animal

flesh wrapped in cellophane, marked
        too expensive. So much I cannot dream

of: sundown at a meadow, late-August
        tranquility folded onto the adipose

of bloated bellies. I have never seen men
        so docile. Perhaps, this is why the lady

horses are most prized. Grandmother
        in the periphery, *strong woman bad.*

Listen to the palpitating of this horse
        heart and I will answer in the language

underneath this skin. Come home from
        the market, empty handed. Daylight

in erasure with the bray of a lost mare
        calling for triumph over superstition.

POEM IN WHICH I CANNOT DRIVE

You imagine me in the driver's seat, not knowing
where I am going. The headlights glare into nothingness
like spitfire eyes, pretending to see the flimsy stars on
the windshield. I memorize the route, a repertoire over
and over again until it becomes as familiar as a visit
to the optometrist. I mistake the flickering streetlights
for passageway, not knowing when to turn right.
Afterwards, I run into cul-de-sacs, endings like
origin stories. You assume I'm afraid of car accidents,
but I have recurring hallucinations about them,
ones where no one rescues me and am left unseen.
I'm tired of imagining my hands on the steering wheel.
Of course, I know better, that people like me can't
drive. A glaucoma patient, myopic. Instead, you are
the driver and I'm a blurred outline in the backseat.
You speed on the highway and my eyes retract
from pressure in the optic nerves. Vision turned
granular. The light from a passing car, filling my eyes
with clouded dust. Then, the background goes completely
dark, even as you drive into the cornea of daybreak.

DEUS EX MACHINA

Let me set the scene for you: Seoul in free fall,
columbariums of teeth accelerating toward
demolition. Do you remember the part where
splintered laments tarmac between my split

lips, tasting of nothing but parasitic skies? Here,
the script marks your entrance as an equal and opposite
reaction. So I attempt chiaroscuro on your palms
to erase the calluses. Fists cupped into a crucible:

oceans basined between tongue-tied confessions
and ruptured lineage. This is the way out: the frayed
railroads mark the rite of passage on your palms.
Remind me how parallel lines don't intersect

and I will abstract myself into a frame of reference
for departure. Your arms still a matrix on mine.

. . .

I choreograph a death in the basement of your womb.
Still in this figure, I sit across the unanswered plot-
lines that palpitate in your trachea. Tell me, our comedy
is an illusion, faces contoured into surrealism.

I no longer want to make-believe. Skyward, strands
of electric cables slash at passenger planes in transit.
Your scalp a planet for lost things: admonitions
for dreaming of immortality, limp cigarette buds

drumming on cracked asphalt like stories torn by shrapnel.
I cannot find a narration for how you stayed silent.
To wish you were a poet in another lifetime, hands knotted
with Goryeo folksong instead of Shakespeare.

Your eyes twitching in the middle of a storm,
climax, tranquility for misplacement.

...

Showdown and I do not ask why I am in the spotlight.
Limbs fixated on fractals of light and throat reeled into
the film. In the audience, I see you mimic a city girl
tethered by American recollections.

Neon signs flickering in reticence. There is no recognition
in this finale, no applause. Perhaps it is the hangul
syllabled between my exhales. Fables margined between
my stardom. Impatient shuffles out of the theater,

an ovation in heartbeats. A gush of adrenaline as
a reminder that I do not belong on this stage. To think
of being a heroine. You, drifting as a fleeting memory
and I wonder if this too, is deception. I praise stories

of tragedy. There is no exit in this cinematography.
The scene will end and we will remain captive.

OF THE WORLDS YOU CAN NAME

You are well-versed in this dialect of invisibility,
        eyes plastered on two halves of the same map.
First, you are faceless. Lost your freedom to the face
        of America. On the bus to downtown Los Angeles,
a tour guide tells you about industrialization, migration,
        Hollywood. The movies are real enough
to make you believe: you cannot be loved in this character.
        The scene smogging your eyes. Isn't it so perfect,
this cityscape? This sunset, choking the girls on the sidewalk.
        Which is to say they become mannequins, immobile.
Limbs thinned to fit into the margins of aspiration.
        Confess, you wanted to be like them. Desire is also
an anomaly. Like any good daughter, you continue walking
        westward. The horizon morphed into the Pacific.
If the waves were silent, you could sing for home.
        A cartographer traces over the other half of your map:
through the looking glass every reflection of your family.
        Mother pounding rice into bamboo leaves,
father chugging mouthfuls of chicken broth. The curves
        of his widow's peak glowing with sweat. This time,
you are searching for a tongue but there is no translation
        for loss. Again, an act of deception. You shove
spoonfuls of cosmetics into your mouth. At least you can be
        beautiful here. Your jawline stitched with delicacy.
Preservation: the morning air like putting on a new hanbok.
        You are visiting your future deathbed, do you realize?
A mourning for the ancestors you have never met.
        Mapping out the outline of illiterate memories,
how nearly you found the landscape of your heritage.

POEM IN WHICH I TALK ABOUT MY DISABILITY
for Constance Merritt

I understand why you talk about
        ghosts in every poem. No, I am
not yet *apprentice ghost* and they
        do not uncover the entrance hall
into this body. Now, I steal
        into the party dressed as *Asian* and
disabled. Someone inquires *where's*
        your costume but there is no oration
for blindness. I can imagine my
        skin scaffolded on a different body,
eyes as mercury in orbit. Even
        in this one, I am unseen. Though
someone is always looking for
        ways to tell me *blind woman is*
less than anything. They tell me
        premeditation does not matter
when taking and I start to question
        my upbringing: *righteousness* as sin,
forgiveness as erasure, *compliance*
        as woman. I will leave this party
unnoticed and smuggle into another
        house, eyeglass in hand. Remind me
I do not have eyes, impaled by
        ghostness in perpetuation. Let
me fist maledictions into locked
        doors on sleepless nights. Blind girl
mistaking braille for celestial bodies.

ENCOUNTER DURING NIGHT OF DEATH

tonight, a girl straggles below streetlights,
the horizon noosing her limbs taut.

away, an apothecary storefront vaults with closure
and the back alleys wind into cul-de-sacs.

she does not return home. instead, the girl trapezes
across monkey bars and scrapes the achromatic skies,

eyeless. armed with fiberglass arrows in this playing ground.
unrelenting to the sickle moon and every reflection of herself

in past lives: vinyl records, broken gods, feet bound by
quiet retributions. she cradles some tight-beaked sparrow

in her palms, cacophonies like the creaks of swing-sets carved
on backbone. oscillating in the world's tongue and someday,

she will fly. call it nostalgia. the quagmire sinking her ambitions.
she pleats each inflated wound into her shirtdress

and constricts dreams in her intestine. shredding memories
from bone marrow, still climbing up the curvature

of a soft embrace. nearby, foxtails ward off the hounds
that bay for her bones. she is here, dissolving in midsummer heat

as the night loosens. in this way, the world meddles with
everything that is not hers. as dawn meets the sockets

where her eyes were, the girl un-sees, eternally burning

SKEDADDLE FOR BLIND GIRL

    A girl vandalizes the walls

              of her epidermis, chiseling
genealogy with an alarming
      deftness. There is no one
           in the vicinity, cordoned
off by her anterior limbs.

Beneath a microscope,
      her eyelids frame her as an imposter,
unscathed by remorse.
      Is this how she's supposed to look
           like? From the periphery of her
eyeglasses, a search party ensues,
      unaware of the victims. Her fractured

magnifying glass refracting the dreams
      augmented by quiet confessions,
           the vitreous body of her eyes
      as foresight. Vessels floating
in aqueous humor. Unwelcomed.
           She wonders if her optic nerves
      lead to an inheritance, if she will find permanence.

Don't tell her to look at the portrait of achromatic faces.
      She can sense the dawn approaching
           but not the shadows
that spiral into cartilage. Instead, the moonlight
      conspires against the watchmen,

an admonition for being sighted.

HAIBUN FOR EVERYTHING THAT DIES THIS SUMMER

It's August again & the world unfurls inside the television screen: record high temperatures, drought, death. Don't remind me that grandfather died within July's stale breath. I do not forgive. Grandmother passes the gourd of water across the congregation of parched throats. This is the last cup & the minutes crawl into the bodies of hours. The supermarket across the street runs out of ice cream & kids throw tantrums across the cracked asphalt, abandoning their youth with such nonchalance. Tell me there used to be a creek. In the present, there is nothing but fossilized departures & the reflection of the scorching sun.

I am landlocked in grandmother's backyard, mouthing an incantation at the apricot tree to hand a blessing. Please, is it going to rain? But the half-bitten leaves wither in the stifling humidity, as if to mock, this is not your place. Grandmother instructs me to catch dragonflies, wait. She clasps their wings with faded thumbprints that run like tributaries across her sallow skin. We are dragonflies, hostages to the heat. I am afraid & the sun claws at my flesh, dried rivermarks streaming across my cheeks. So this is affection. Knees scarred from wildfires gone awry like this was never planned.

Twilight & I watch the moths navigate for the cold-blooded moonlight, crickets strumming their guitars, sprawled across the desert. The deboned constellations hang crooked, bleached white from the dry spell. Grandmother tells me they are my ancestors & I delineate their lineage across the skymap. The weather forecast maps itself onto the planets, extreme weather imminent. Even the night cannot fool the sun, relentless. In someplace far off, the yolk of the sun cracks onto the horizon, heat waves gushing into the thirsty ocean. Washed-up bodies reek of hyperthermia & I forget

>   I am still alive. The sun
>   surrendering nothing
>   to the wreckage

GHAZAL FOR K

Last summer, grandmother moved to California, bone-dried and thinned
like seaweed on the kitchen counter. She asks why I have not thinned,

fattened instead like a whale ready for slaughter, and blames the grease
on miguk food. I want to tell her I am not American, hangul thinned

into the back of my tongue and unreceptive to the stench of modernity.
The only word I remember in Korean is sijang, hunger. Oceans thinned

by extinction, harbors split by upturned boats, famine kneeling in front
of my bruised mouth. Grandmother says sijang can mean market, thinned

aisles of canned tuna and fake kimchi, the commodities of my past I want
forgotten. What remains of my weekly allowance, I squander on thinned

cityscape portraits and white pearl necklaces. This is why grandmother
mistakes me for an American girl, future Hollywood star. Foolish, thinned

with dreams about origin stories. Yesterday, it was about a father aspiring
to be a mayor, also sijang. Today, it is an elegy for my father, thinned

white hairs as trench lines. Grandmother reminds me of the Korean
wars I have not seen, dynasties wrecked by bullets, history thinned

inside the barrel of a rifle. The summer of my father's death, grandmother
swapped his body with an aircraft, propelled it towards the Pacific-thinned

waves, escaping west. Midway, shipwrecks invaded his body, so I learned
to spill his ashes on Californian seabeds before I had known the thinned

calluses on his hands. This summer, grandmother moves back, says loss
is too foreign. Alone, I unlearn jeonjaeng, war, the memories thinning.

DISAPPEARING ACT

In the morning we're found standing on the patio by the seaside. Summertime up to our waistlines. This is where we begin, submerged in the first aphorism of Hippocrates; *yes, my father is a doctor* and *no,* I do not harbor such ambitions. Greetings morph themselves into sermons and we are transported back to Sunday afternoons. Picture me as a child. Demented chronographs jutting out of the asymmetric pockets of my duffle coat. Time warped by a curious presence. We learn to vanish from this timeframe. There is a ritual we have yet to uncover,

an astrological coincidence you cannot map out. The stars blink in ciphers, we answer with morse-code signals while switching planes for planets. You bring out a telescope from the basement and orient your eye towards larger objects. We learn to hide among apparitions that hover over fluorescent lights in this ghost town. In this land, everyone aspires to be invisible without knowing what they're hiding from. *Is this how you want to end up?* You tell me not to look for answers. You meant to say *no*. It ends with a projectile gone awry.

                                                    I am your next target.

OCCLUDER

I am the next patient. The door / to the optometrist's office / opens but I refuse to go inside. / I've been here many times, / a ritual. The eye doctor shines / a light into my eyes and I'm afraid / he can trace the dream / I had last night. One where / ghosts float like vitreous in my eyes. / A vision test to prove my / probable existence. Next, I must / play a guessing game. *Choose, E or B?* / Concerned, the optometrist / considers other options. *What about braille?* I will become / specks of stardust, scratched out / of parchment canvases. The eye / chart glares back as encrypted / letters. I seek exit labels that / ignore my condition, the only / way out, unsighted.

MONOCHROMACY

We're at the movies and the scene unfolds in
        Casablanca monochrome. Now comes the climax:
a man digs up an eye from the surface of his limbs,
        soiled with blood. He plays the villain and the victim.
You flinch at this grotesque sight and I see

the red of blood as silvered water. The theater burns
        in its technicolor haze and I wish I could evaporate
into the obsidian of your eyes, reflecting a useless
        sheen of gray. The man on the screen loses his eye
in a vintage store and the audience whimpers in pity.

How naive. You reach for the almost-empty bag
        of popcorn and find an eyeball inside. You are
in this act as the victim. The villain towers over
        like an impending storm. Forgive me for being unable
to differentiate tears from dew, hair from forestry.

Your eyes, the brightest shade of fear. I see nothing.
        I leave you inside the pigmented cinematography
of your fate. You keep asking me if I can see the blood
        on your palms. I don't. You forget I am colorblind
and something inside me loves this colorless ending.

FIREWORK GIRLS

Firework girls sashay down the sidewalks
with ankles swollen like cherry bombs.
Firework girls don't trip over candy wrappers
on the floor—instead, they throw fire-
crackers into the air, then run away
from the explosion. Meanwhile,
an army of explosive boys with drumstick
legs beat on the tarmac, a parade to celebrate
the beginnings of something greater
than themselves. Meanwhile, I lay supine
on a football stadium, humming anthems
my father used to sing, ready to be trampled
by a band of marchers wielding their
trombones and cymbals like weapons.
I'm at a party full of firework girls
but am the only one wearing jeans,
the only one with glasses thicker than fences.
The paparazzi thinks I'm exotic enough
to live captive in his photo gallery,
so he angles his camera at my eyes
and gets angry when I'm not looking
straight at him. All I see is the negative space
of his body, and even his body is a mirage
I create with my eyes closed. I am not like
firework girls, which is to say I am more silent,
more polite, more docile. Firework girls
don't understand what it means to live
off hand-me-down blouses and wallets
without credit cards, just green cards
that will expire next month. Firework girls
wear contact lenses as cosmetics; I wear them
for survival. Firework girls raise their glasses
in cheer, and one of the blond girls
extends a glass of tequila in my direction,

an invitation to play pretend.
Here, a masquerade of bodies basked
in lavish light. Firework girls don't
understand the tiger in my mother,
the way she flares up when I mention
the American way of living. At home,
celebration is silent, all five of us pressed into
a dining table for four, too scared to turn on
the TV just to see another shooting, another
headline with eight Asians dead, six of them
women. At home, we eat rice cakes
as a substitute for burgers, even on days
like today when we can call ourselves American.
At home, we forget, then remember everything
in bursts, mother rocking my brother to sleep
with Korean folk songs while I try to unstitch
them from my ears. Outside, the party never ends,
fireworks booming in the distance, always
taken for bullets. In the end, the firework girls
will burst into sparks of light and I will be
the only one remaining in this landscape,
waiting for the slow-jazz dawn to rise. I am alone
but not uninvited, no longer afraid of illusions,
fireworks, my own girlhood. When tomorrow
becomes today, I welcome myself
into the party, humming melodies of rebirth.

FACELESS ELEGY
>for San Francisco / Prague / Seoul
>after Lily Zhou / Cathy Linh Che

In California, the skyscrapers have never met God, only ghosts.
I've seen mirages of my dead body laid bare, as the ends of a highway
morph into a cul-de-sac. I am not a girl who lies but one who has
never known the truth, memories of home relapsing like pale waves.
Let me confess: if only I can silver my voice into static, if only the city
streets can dissolve the bones between my name, I will love the way
San Francisco is dying. I will love the broken horses on carousels,
sea lions jutting out from the ocean like cavities, caricatures of my past
life on sale for five dollars. I yearn to visit my next life,

so I board a flight to Prague, landlocked with suitcases that reek of brine
and fever dreams where crabs wear my face, a one-person masquerade
where I am an outsider. Out in the city, the medieval clock forgets
the value of its own hands, reverses history until there is nothing
left to mourn for, not even the martyred ghosts hiding behind cathedral
arches. One night, I climb skyscrapers to find my ghost sitting alone
at an al fresco bar, face swollen with doses of champagne. All I want
is to prove that I am not the obedient girl I used to be, that I, too,
have never known God. Ghost, another word for erasure.

Tell me, there are still hymns in the glass's reflection, calling me home.
Tell me I am still beautiful in all the ways a funeral can be. The bodies
stilted against the wall, fatigued by sleepless nights. The men playing
hwatu, their bellies erupting with greed and soju. The mother at the altar,
rubbing her face with tears. In Korea, funerals are more for the living
than the dead, and I think it's romantic. The guests will burn incense
in front of my self-portrait, framed with chrysanthemums.

They will forget my face, then their own. I write the same poem on different faces, in different cities. In Seoul, I cannot distinguish tree trunks from telephone poles, phantoms from smog. When it rains, every droplet on my face turns into eyes, and I should have gazed into those eyes, everyone's eyes—back when I was alive.

THERE IS NO RENAISSANCE HERE

and that is to say the vestige will haunt you
        tonight. Your rubbled body submerged

in starlight. Take pillar as bone and arch
        as the curvature of your spine. You cannot talk

about bodies and you will realize this poem
        is no longer about you. Neither is it about

the intricate archeology of a self-righteous
        daughter. At times, you imagine what it means

to rebuild antiquity. Your father an architect
        in a past life, kneeling over converging parallel

lines and Brunelleschi's dome. Wonder why
        he was praised for mimicking archaic as if he

could bring back the deceased. You decipher
        revolutions from cryptic dreams. It's deceptive,

and you will remember dawn as rebirth.
        Master stoicism and perhaps you are not human

anymore. Shapeshift into Michaelangelo's
        David, pose as artwork. You will be loved

and nothing more. Meanwhile, a historian
        will confuse marble for creation, silence for

survival. You will learn to replace punctured
        history as erasure, framed into a facade of illusion.

IN A DREAM, WE ALL LOSE OUR SIGHT

So much happened after you left the house. For one thing, we found a dead rabbit in the front yard and covered it with rain. We're reminded that skeletons can be soft, haunting the damp fractures of our ankles. Later that evening, its ghost scampered off to the neighbor's storage cellar and was never sighted again. The peculiarity of this disappearing act. A warning we did not catch. Instead, we fox-hunt for your beaded rabbit eyes. Before going to bed, we prey you into our dreams. Both still alive and visible in the saturated nightlife.

You're in the dream but we don't see you. At first, we blame it on the dimness, but soon realize it's our eyes. The tapered slits like lightning bolts on a faceless topography. We're going blind and it doesn't make sense. If a storm can spit out a language in your absence, why should we summon you back into our vision? If braille isn't a language, why does it need a translation? These questions hang unanswered on our eyelashes and we don't want them to sag onto our pupils. Nystagmus eyes convulsing like chattering teeth. An aching for the words we never told you.

In another dream, we get a phone call from the optician about your next appointment. They recommend that you get a new pair of glasses, but we decline. Anyways, you're not the one needing eyewear. It's us. We try to carve our eyes onto the walls, expecting to see. In yet another dream, we dilate our pupils to find out the possible causes for the sudden loss of sight. The evidence gravitates toward you, admit it. The light refracted by the scratched surface of your lens.

When you told us we would eventually be sightless, you probably had hyperopia and saw the distant future. That is to say you did not recognize anything near you. Not the distance between the craters where our eyes used to fit into. Not the radioactive decay of your partial eyesight. How far away are you in the first place? Nightly, our sight vanishes into the storage cellar of your vitreous humor. It's not funny anymore, the dreams welling in our visual field.

POEM IN WHICH MY DISABILITY TALKS ABOUT ME

At the art museum, the paintings turn into eyes.
        Eyes that have only seen perfection.
I call it sacrifice—my disability calls it beauty.

                How unfamiliar it is to watch
the crowds staring back into my eyes.
        I have never made eye contact before,
not even with my disability.

                Not even with myself,
my pixelated face blurring away the cracks on my glasses.
        I am not guilty of forgetting;
I'm just learning to see myself in a mirror.
                Learning to love my disability.

            Sometimes, I can see trajectories of light
on the darkscapes of my eyelids
        and I believe in those moments:
believe I can cup my fingers around my disability and tell her it's okay.

                In the operating room,
the surgeons remove the lens in my eyes
        and my disability cries in the waiting room,
prays that I will have perfect eyesight in my next life.
    Someday, I will learn to praise my eyes
the way my disability idolizes me.
        Someday, I will tell my disability
    I'd want to keep her in my next life.

              I no longer fit into the museum exhibitions,
and the crowds no longer gaze at my flaws. Look,
        I should have gazed into those eyes,
    everyone's eyes, the glamor of them all.

ACKNOWLEDGEMENTS

L(EYE)GHT is a landscape of my identity as a poet. It is for the times I've spent wanting to be someone else, desperately trying to hide, finding comfort in wildness. This book has given me a new way to make eye contact with the world, and I want to extend my endless gratitude to everyone who has made eye contact back:

To the editors of the following journals who have published my poems, often in earlier forms:

> "SHATTERED" in *The Adroit Journal*
> "BRAILLET" in *Whale Road Review*
> "WHAT NOT TO EXPECT AT A KOREAN SUPERMARKET" in *Gulf Stream Magazine*
> "SUPERMARKET HORSE" in *Longleaf Review*
> "POEM IN WHICH I TALK ABOUT MY DISABILITY" in *Glass: A Journal of Poetry*
> "ENCOUNTER DURING NIGHT OF DEATH" in *Cosmonauts Avenue*
> "SKEDADDLE FOR BLIND GIRL" in *Petrichor Magazine*
> "HAIBUN FOR EVERYTHING THAT DIES THIS SUMMER" in *perhappened magazine*
> "DISAPPEARING ACT" in *Red Rock Review*
> "THERE IS NO RENAISSANCE HERE" in *Wildness Journal*

To my mother who has involuntarily become the subject of many of my works, and has shown me boundless support for my poems despite only having read them through google translate. And to the rest of my family for the road trips and dinner table conversations that led to this book.

To my friends around the world who have slowly seen me evolve from a math nerd to a poet, but also seen my obsession with polar bears, Kdramas, and all-nighters. Special shoutout to Miye for translating her doodled sketches into the most dazzling cover artwork ever.

To my past and present English teachers who have read more of my writing than anyone else in the world, altered my daily thought process, and called me a "good" writer even when I could never see myself as one. You are my role models.

To my mentors: S for giving me the inspiration to write about my visual impairment at a time when I felt alone in representing that narrative, C for being the first person to congratulate me on every piece of poetry news I receive, and M and N for transforming my poems into radically strange and luminous ways.

To the brush I grabbed during doljabi—a Korean tradition that foretells a baby's future—on my first birthday. The brush symbolizes a writer, and as an avid believer in fate, I think this was all meant to be.

To you, who has devoured every word in this book and made it to the end. My eternal love goes out to you for believing in a pandemic-born teen poet who started with nothing. I promise to write more poems for you.

Jessica Kim
April 2022

ABOUT THE AUTHOR

Jessica Kim is a Korean-American and disabled poet. She is the 2021 Youth Poet Laureate of Los Angeles, a YoungArts Finalist in Poetry, and a Commended Foyle Young Poet. Aside from writing poetry, she serves as the Editor-in-Chief of *The Lumiere Review* and *Polyphony Lit*. Find more of her work at www.jessicakimwrites.weebly.com.

www.ingramcontent.com/pod-product-compliance
Lightning Source LLC
Chambersburg PA
CBHW060224050426
42446CB00013B/3156